from confetti.co.uk
don't get married without us…

First published in 2001 by Octopus Publishing Group,
2–4 Heron Quays, London, E14 4JP
www.conran-octopus.co.uk

ISBN 1 84091 227 8

Publishing Director Lorraine Dickey;
Creative Director Leslie Harrington;
Senior Editor Katey Day; *Copy-editor* Helen Ridge;
Designer Megan Smith; *Production Director* Zoë Fawcett

Contents

Weddings sometimes seem like the mystical domain of women. They've reputedly always known exactly what they want from the big day since they were six years old. Somehow they also seem to know how to organize everyone, as well as what to do and say, not to mention knowing exactly what they and a number of assorted bridesmaids are going to wear.

INTRODUCTION

So, as a man, what's your role? If you're the groom, you know you'll be playing a pretty important part in this day – but what exactly are you meant to do? And if you're the proud father, are you meant to be just an open cheque book – but what's your role if you're not paying?

And what if you're just an innocent
bystander – a poor unfortunate who,
by no greater crime on your part than
a long association with the groom, has
been hauled into active service as the best
man or an usher? This little book aims to
answer all these questions and more,
as well as giving you a selection of top
tips for all men at weddings!

Above all else, don't lose sight of the fact that you're meant to be enjoying yourself (yes, even while 100 people stare at you as you desperately try to remember who you are meant to toast at the end of your speech!). So if you're stumped about planning a stag night, perplexed by the preparations or just lost for words when it comes to making a speech, then read on.

The groom

So, here it is, the biggest day of your life. Perhaps you haven't thought about it in this way before but, come the day itself, you will! Whatever the size of wedding, there is a lot to consider – before, during and after the actual ceremony.

The proposal

If you've been stepping out for what seems a lifetime already or you've been living together for God knows how long, there comes a time when it's simply rude not to have popped the question. Your proposal is the first step towards a childhood dream that your girlfriend will have entertained since the playground. Even the coolest cat goes to pieces when her ideal man drops down on to one knee.

Pre-wedding organization

In terms of organizing 'the big day' itself, there's a lot to be said for hanging back and letting the bride and her family bond over the wedding preparations, while you merely approve their decisions and referee the slanging matches. What's more, if her family is paying for the wedding, it's really only fair to let them lead the planning.

Having your say

It's your day too, don't be railroaded into a wedding that isn't you. Our advice is to save putting your foot down for the things you really don't want, rather than arguing over every buttonhole. Otherwise, you'll have a miserable run-up to the big day. You might also want to state early on if there are any specific things you'd like to decide yourself or take responsibility for.

Paying for the wedding

Generally, the groom pays for:

- the wedding rings
- the hire and cost of his own clothes
- all church/register office expenses
- the bride's bouquet
- the bridesmaids' flowers
- buttonholes for the male members of the wedding party
- presents for the best man, ushers and bridesmaids
- the honeymoon

The wedding rings

One of the very first tasks is to buy the wedding rings. It's a good idea to look at these when you buy the engagement ring, as your bride will eventually wear both together on the third finger of her left hand, and they should match. Most couples go shopping for the rings together, or order them from a ring designer.

The wedding rings

Wedding rings are usually made from white, red or yellow gold or platinum. The design can take many forms: it can be of any width or weight and may be engraved on the inner surface with the couple's initials or a suitable inscription.

The wedding rings

Whether you want to wear a wedding ring yourself is a question of personal preference – and that of your bride! Customs vary all over the world.

The stag party

It's the task of your best man to make all the arrangements for the stag party. If you have strong ideas on what you want to do – or definitely don't want to do – let him know firmly and early on. Holding your stag party right before your wedding is to be avoided – give yourself time to recover!

Choosing the groomsmen

The groom chooses his best man and ushers, who are also known as 'groomsmen' because they are your people! Don't be pressured into having someone you don't want as your best man and, obviously, avoid choosing someone who: used to go out with your future wife; is likely to let you down on the day in some way (by getting drunk or making a rude speech); is no good with parents or has little sense of occasion.

What to wear

If your wedding is formal and you want the
men to wear morning dress, then you need
to arrange with your best man to hire the
outfits. Once you've tried them on and
made your choice, get the booking in
writing and agree who will return your suit
while you are on your honeymoon. If the
wedding is less formal, buy an appropriate
suit in good time and let your attendants
know so they can wear something similar.

Buttonholes

You will need to arrange for a florist to make the buttonholes for you and your attendants – this can usually be done by the same florist who creates the bouquets for the bride and bridesmaids, but check to make sure. The buttonholes need to be brought to the church early and with pins so that they can be fixed in place.

The wedding rehearsal

It is customary — and very sensible — to have a rehearsal of the ceremony shortly before the event. The celebrant will take you through your part in the ceremony and answer any questions.

The night before the wedding

It is considered unlucky for the bridegroom
to set eyes on the bride the night before
the wedding ceremony, so even couples
who live together tend to spend the night
before their wedding apart. Beware of
celebrating your 'last night of freedom'
down the pub – a hangover is the last thing
you need on your wedding day!

The wedding day

It's usually up to the groom and best man to get themselves to the church on time, so ask your best man to sort out reliable transport. It might be handy to have the number of a local taxi firm, just in case!

The wedding day

The start of the day will be dictated by what time you are getting married. If you are having an afternoon or evening wedding, try to relax by getting in a round of golf or a game of tennis. If you are having a morning wedding, remember to eat breakfast – it's a long time till lunch!

The wedding morning checklist

- Do you have your buttonhole?
- Does the best man have the rings?
- Do you have a crib sheet of events?
- Do you have your speech notes?
- Do you have the 'thank-you' gifts?
- Do you have some spare change in case of emergencies?

The wedding morning checklist

- Has the luggage for your first night and honeymoon — including documents, tickets and passport — been delivered to your first-night hotel?
- Do you have your going-away outfit?
- Do you have your going-away car keys, if you're driving?

At the church

The bridegroom and best man should arrive at the church about half an hour before the service and wait for the bride either in the vestry or seated in the front pew on the right-hand side of the church. At a given signal, the bridegroom takes his place at the chancel steps before the altar, with the best man standing to his right. Then the bride will begin that long, long walk up the aisle.

At the register office

Before the ceremony, the registrar meets with the couple to confirm that all the correct information has been filed. During the ceremony, you are both asked to make declarations that you are legally free to marry and, provided there is no legal impediment, you exchange marriage vows. This can be accompanied by the exchange of rings. After signing the register, the bride and groom are usually invited to lead their wedding party out.

During the ceremony

Although the minister or registrar usually asks you to repeat his or her words when the time comes to give your vows, learning the lines beforehand will enable you to deliver them much more confidently. It's so much more romantic to be gazing at your bride during the ceremony than looking for a prompt from the minister or registrar!

Leaving the ceremony

Once you are officially husband and wife,
you must both sign the register. This takes
place in the vestry if you marry in a church,
or at the front of the room if you marry in
a register office. After receiving
congratulations and greetings from your
witnesses, you give your bride your left arm
and, together, you lead the bridal
procession down the aisle, or out of the
register office, to end the ceremony.

At the reception

You should welcome your guests as they arrive at the reception and mingle with them, introducing your bride to members of your family and friends whom she has not already met. Alternatively, you may stand in a formal line to greet each guest as they file into the dining area.

THE GROOM

The groom's speech

The bridegroom's speech is supposed to be a reply to the toast to 'the bride and groom', made by the bride's father. Its primary purpose is to thank your bride's parents for both their daughter and for the wedding, and also to thank your parents and guests. You may like to remember absent friends. You should finish your speech by thanking the bridesmaids and proposing a toast to them.

The speech checklist

• Thank the father of the bride (and any other speakers) for their speeches. You might want to say that you won't let the father of the bride down and how proud you are to be his son-in-law.

• Make some topical remarks about how successful the wedding has been so far.

• Thank all the people who have helped with the wedding and give them their gifts.

• Thank everyone for coming and send good wishes to those unable to attend.

THE GROOM

The speech checklist
- Describe the background to the happy day. Mention how you and your bride first met. Tell a few amusing or embarrassing stories — the more humiliating to you, the funnier for everyone else!
- Say something addressed exclusively to your bride about how happy you are to be marrying her.
- Say a few words about the best man.
- Conclude with a toast to the bridesmaids from you and your new wife.

Thank-you presents

It is traditional for the bride and groom to exchange gifts with each other on their wedding day. The bridegroom also buys thank-you presents for the bridesmaids and pageboys. This is often jewellery, but it could be any kind of memento.

For some present ideas, try our gift shop at:
www.confetti.co.uk/men/p34

Thank-you presents

As well as thanking the bridesmaids,
most couples like to thank both sets
of parents, the best man and the ushers.
Presenting bouquets to the mothers is
usual practice. Don't forget anyone who
has made a special contribution to the
celebrations, such as the friend who made
the bride's dress, created the wedding cake
or played the organ.

After the speeches

After the speeches, you and your new wife usually cut the cake. You may start the dancing with a romantic 'first dance', too, after which you are free to enjoy your reception as you wish. But remember that you are one of the reasons people are there, so try to mingle.

Leaving the reception

If you're being ultra-traditional, you and
your bride will disappear at some point in
the evening to change and then reappear
to bid your guests farewell before 'going
away'. If you plan to party until the bitter
end, be polite and warn your older guests
– they were brought up to think it rude
to leave a reception before the bride
and groom!

Leaving the reception

Remember to book your first night's accommodation at a local hotel, and make sure you have arranged for a taxi to take you there from the reception. You might want to plan a romantic surprise in your hotel room, such as candles, soft music, champagne or flowers.

The honeymoon

The groom traditionally arranges (and pays for) the honeymoon, sometimes keeping the location a secret, even from the bride. Perhaps there is a special place she has always wanted to visit? Bear in mind that surprises can backfire, though, so before you plan an energetic sports holiday, check that your bride wasn't expecting two weeks relaxing on a deserted island.

The best man

As best man, you need to be an
organizer, a troubleshooter,
an entertainer, a friend and, come
the stag night, a chaperon.

Overseeing the proceedings

The best man is one of the key figures in the wedding ritual. Not only do you play an important role in the weeks leading up to the event (particularly on the groom's side), but you also oversee the whole day itself in the capacity of 'Master of Ceremonies'.

The ideal best man

The perfect best man should probably
have the following qualities:

- reliability
- people skills
- a good sense of humour
- strong public-speaking skills
- ability to stay calm under pressure
- ability to get on with the bride
  and her family

The ideal best man

If you're really up for the job of best man
but don't think you can muster all the ideal
qualities, don't worry. The entertainment
value of weddings is often greatly improved
by the best man's deficiency in any of the
departments mentioned on the left!

Pre-wedding chat

Arrange a 'family huddle'. Get together with the groom, bride and her parents to find out how you can help prepare for the wedding. The earlier the chat, the better, so that everyone is given the chance to have their say, and jobs and duties can be allocated. Create a pleasant environment for the conversation – a meal out, perhaps – and explain beforehand the point of the meeting, so that everyone has the opportunity to gather their thoughts.

Visit the venues

If possible, you should accompany the bride and groom on a visit to their chosen ceremony and reception venues. Make a note of such details as how long the various journeys take, the locations of entrances and exits, parking facilities, and so on — all the things that will help to ensure the smooth flow of guests on the day.

Organizing the ushers

Traditionally, the groom and best man get together to choose the ushers. The role of the ushers is largely restricted to assisting guests to their seats for the wedding ceremony. As best man, you need to ensure they recognize the key family members and are generally charming and helpful. Ushers should also make sure that the seats reserved for close family are not 'invaded' by other guests.

Organizing the transport

You may be asked to arrange transport for the wedding day. An average order would be two cars from the bridal home to the ceremony venue and three from the church to the reception – the third car obviously being for the newlyweds. Crucially, it's your job to get the groom to the venue on time and in one piece, for which you may prefer to rely on your own transport. It's a good idea to take maps of the venues as well as a mobile phone to help any lost guests.

Organizing the stag party

It's down to you to organize the stag night, the groom's traditional farewell to the single life. In preparing your send-off, resist the pressure to live up – or down – to the abundance of stag-night horror stories. Sure, you may want the groom to be the butt of a few jokes, but the stag night should ultimately be seen as an affectionate celebration, rather than a gruesome ordeal

When to hold the stag party

Nowadays, the night before the wedding is considered a definite no-no for the stag party. The best time is at least a week before the big day and, if possible, over the same weekend as the bride's hen party — this means the couple won't lose two weekends together in the crucial last few planning weeks before the wedding.

Where to hold the stag party

When organizing the stag party, you'll also need to think about the party location. Do most of the groom's friends live in one area, or is there a central town that's easily accessible for everyone? And don't forget to ask the groom for names and contact numbers of any people you don't know.

Funding the stag party

The stag party costs – including those of the groom, who shouldn't have to fork out for anything himself – should be divvied out among the group. If it's a pub crawl you're planning, sort out the money before people get too drunk – ask everyone to contribute towards a kitty at the start of the evening.

Pace yourself

On the day of the stag party, your main
challenge is to keep the momentum going,
so pace the events. If a lot of alcohol is
involved, don't let everyone (especially
the groom!) get too drunk too soon –
plan a meal in a cheap restaurant as part
of the celebrations or organize food to
be laid on in a pub.

A sight for sore eyes

Take a camera with you to the stag party for some memorable shots, or a video camera to record all the live action! And don't forget it's your job to make sure people don't play jokes on the groom that may not seem funny in the morning – such as dyeing his hair blue or sending him off on a cross-channel ferry!

Stag party ideas

For clubbers: book a party bus tour of nightclubs – the price for these usually includes wine and beer on the bus, plus all entry fees. For boy racers: choose from a day at Brands Hatch, pushing a Ferrari to its limits, or tearing across rough terrain in a 4x4, or competing against your mates at go-karting. For modern couples: have a joint hen and stag night, or invite an equal number of friends for a weekend at a country house.

What to wear for the wedding

Traditionally, the best man, the father of the bride, ushers and pageboys all take their lead from the outfit chosen by the groom. If morning dress is to be hired, it's a good idea to try and arrange for all the fittings to be done together or at least by the same supplier. Usually, each individual will pay for his own clothes hire.

The wedding morning

You will have a lot to do on the wedding day itself – so much, in fact, that you probably won't even have time to get nervous about your speech (as if…!). Prior to the ceremony, it's traditional to pop round to the bride's to pick up buttonholes, telegrams, last-minute messages and any final instructions about seating arrangements, and so on.

The morning checklist

- Make sure the bride and groom have their honeymoon kit: luggage, tickets, passports and money.
- Pick up buttonholes for the groom, yourself and the ushers.
- Check final arrangements: service sheets, hired cars and photographer.
- The rings! The rings!
- Otherwise, just be there for the groom: calm his nerves, make sure he eats something – whatever he wants or needs.

During the ceremony

As best man, you, of course, will have arrived at the church or register office early with the groom, giving yourself plenty of time to check that the service sheets and buttonholes are to hand, that the ushers are fully instructed, and to check (and check again!) for the rings.

During the ceremony

Once you've reassured yourself that everything's running smoothly, make your way serenely to your appointed place next to the groom at the front of the church or register office on the right-hand side. Whatever you are feeling inside, do not look nervous – the groom has enough on his mind.

During the ceremony

A few minutes before the bride's entrance and procession, you and the groom will stand to take your places at the chancel steps, or in front of the registrar. (You are always to the groom's right.) Follow the service attentively, since your next job is the biggest of all: to produce the wedding ring on cue for the groom.

At the church

Towards the end of a church service, you're likely to escort the chief bridesmaid to the signing of the register and, if necessary, act as a witness. In the concluding procession, your place is after the bridal attendants (bridesmaids, pageboys, and the like), on the right of the chief bridesmaid – your opposite number. The best man is also responsible for making sure any outstanding fees for the service, organist and bellringers are paid.

At the register office

Your role at the register office is very similar to that in a church. If no emergencies need attending to, then make your way to the right of the groom, who stands on the right of the bride. If the bride and groom have decided to exchange rings in the ceremony, be alert to the moment when you have to hand them over. You may be required to be one of the two witnesses who sign the register with the bride and groom at the end of the ceremony.

At the register office

If there are any fees due, they will be paid at this stage. As with a church wedding, the groom or father of the bride will normally provide the money, but it is the best man's job to make sure it is handed over to the registrar. Ensure you have collected the money from the appropriate person beforehand.

Leaving the ceremony

Once the bride and groom have left
the church or register office, your role
as master of ceremonies kicks in. You
are on hand to help the photographer
arrange the various group shots. You stand
by to see the happy couple into their car
and make sure – with the help of the
ushers – that everyone has a lift to
the reception. Traditionally, the best man
makes his own way to the reception with
the bridal attendants.

At the reception

If the reception begins with a receiving line, make sure you're standing after the bridal attendants. Unless there's a toastmaster, the best man acts as continuity announcer, directs guests to their seats, introduces the speeches and announces the cake-cutting. Your speech, which traditionally comes last, is usually prefaced by the reading of cards, telegrams and messages from guests unable to attend. It also incorporates a reply on behalf of the bridesmaids.

The best man's speech

Start preparing your speech several weeks before the day. If you're stuck for stories or ideas, ring around friends and relatives, who'll be only too delighted to have their say! Bear in mind that the traditional function of your speech is to give some background to the groom for the benefit of the bride's side of the family.

The speech checklist

- Thank the bride and groom for their gifts, and compliment the 'team' of bridesmaids, ushers and pageboys.
- Read out any telegrams and other messages from invited guests unable to attend the wedding.

The speech checklist

- Near the start of your speech, you might want to tell some behind-the-scenes stories about preparing for the wedding — especially any amusing incidents or narrowly averted disasters.
- Make a point of addressing the couple, and of talking to and about the bride. Too many best man's speeches almost overlook her entirely.

The speech checklist

- And so to the traditional main task: embarrassing the groom. Your material should be funny without being nasty, risqué without being offensive. Props are often used here, and stories from the stag night often crop up, too.

- It can seem like a good idea to mention past relationships, but tread carefully. The golden rule: if there's a chance it might upset the bride, leave it out.

The speech checklist

- Leaven the mockery with some sincerity. Talk about how you met the groom, how you came to be best mates, how much you really think of him, your perspective on the growing relationship between bride and groom, and give them your best wishes for their future together.

The speech checklist

- If you need to give the guests any information about the reception, include this after your main speech.
- Conclude your speech with a toast to the bride and groom.

The father of the bride

Your little girl has grown up and is now getting married. It's the day you've always dreaded, and not just because you'll have to remortgage the house! But what exactly is your role during the preparations and on the big day itself?

How much involvement?

Your role is to support your daughter
in every way. Usually, this also means
financially! So what's new? Some fathers
choose to participate in all aspects of the
wedding preparations, while others prefer
to stand back and allow the groom, bride
and her mother to make the arrangements.
Either way is fine. And, frankly, your
daughter may have already decided what
she wants you to do!

Paying for the wedding

Nowadays, the cost of even the most
modest wedding can be astronomical.
A wise father will set his budget as early as
possible and advise the couple as to what
he is able, and prepared, to spend.

Setting a budget

If you establish your budget early on, there can be no misunderstandings. The couple can then plan accordingly and decide on their priorities.

For a full breakdown of the average cost of each wedding item, register for a confetti.co.uk budget planner at:
www.confetti.co.uk/men/p75

Bills, bills, bills!

Traditionally, the bride's family pays for:

- engagement and wedding press announcements
- the bride's and bridesmaids' dresses
- outfits for the bride's mother and father
- flowers for the church and reception (groom pays for bouquets and buttonholes)
- photographer
- most of the transport
- wedding stationery
- the reception – the big expense!

Help from the groom's family

Although it is traditional for the bride's parents to pay for the wedding, the groom's parents are often pleased to contribute in some way, so that the couple can have the wedding they really want. However, this is not a foregone conclusion, and you should not expect the groom's parents to share the bill or be offended if they don't offer to do so.

Sharing the costs

If the groom's parents tactfully make an offer to contribute to the cost of the wedding and you are happy for them to do so, then make a list of who's paying for what as soon as possible, to avoid any misunderstandings. Tread carefully, though. Ask them first what they had in mind!

Stepping back

If the bride and groom are paying for everything themselves, what does the father of the bride do? Here are some ideas:

- Support: offer to take your daughter to her dress fittings, collect the wedding stationery, and so on.
- Information: make sure you make the addresses of all the relatives being invited available to the couple.
- Look after the mother of the bride – this is an important job on the day!

What to wear

The groom usually feels quite strongly about whether he wants the men in the wedding party to wear morning dress or lounge suits. You should expect to be consulted, but if your views differ wildly from those of your daughter's fiancé, you might have to give in – eventually!

Hiring a suit

Groom, best man, ushers, bride's father and groom's father should all be dressed similarly. Unless you already have a suit of your own, consult with the groom about hiring similar outfits, so that you achieve a coordinated effect on the day. Remember that a hired suit needs to be fitted and ordered well in advance to ensure that it's ready for the big day.

For details of the confetti.co.uk online suit hire, go to: www.confetti.co.uk/menatweddings/p81

Wedding day checklist

- Your most important task is to support your daughter and calm her nerves.
- You need to make sure the cars arrive to take the bridesmaids, mother of the bride and other members of the family to the ceremony.
- Above all, you need to get your daughter to the church or register office on time!

Travelling to the ceremony

When helping your daughter into the bridal car, make sure that her fabulous dress or outfit is not crushed or creased. Also, remember to take a large umbrella in the car with you in case it's raining when you reach the wedding venue – you want the bride to look as dignified as possible when she gets out of the car.

At the church

If the wedding takes place in a church, you will walk your daughter slowly up the aisle and, in some church ceremonies, place her hand in the groom's as you 'give her away'. Once the couple are officially husband and wife, it is usual for you to escort the groom's mother to the vestry for the signing of the register. After this, you walk back down the aisle with the groom's mother on your right-hand side, following the bride's mother and the groom's father.

At the register office

If the marriage is taking place at a register office, it is up to your daughter to decide whether she wants to enter the room accompanied by you or perhaps her chief attendant, since there is no real etiquette involved. As her father, however, you are the usual choice. Traditionally, you sit in the front row during the ceremony on the left-hand side.

Leaving the ceremony

Obviously, you don't ride with your daughter to the reception but take your place, usually in the third car, following the bridesmaids and best man, or, in the fourth car, with the groom's parents.

Receiving guests at the reception

At the reception, you and the mother of the bride are the hosts. If you are to welcome guests in a formal receiving line, your place is second in the line, after the bride's mother. If the bride and groom prefer to welcome everyone on their own, your job is to mingle with the guests, circulate and make introductions.

The father of the bride's speech

Speeches usually take place after the meal has finished and prior to the cutting of the cake. Traditionally, the father of the bride is the first speaker – apart from a brief introduction from the best man – so your speech is a sort of scene-setter for what's to come.

The father of the bride's speech

In your speech, you'll probably want to talk about your daughter, as – again, as tradition would have it – you hand her over from your care into that of her new partner.

The father of the bride's speech
Fathers and daughters are always thought
to have very special relationships but, in
your speech, try to avoid the clichés and
talk realistically and affectionately about
your own specific relationship – its ups
and downs, the funny foibles and the
silly stories.

The father of the bride's speech

Your speech also gives you the chance to welcome the groom officially into your family, so you may want to talk about how you first got to know him and what your first impressions were. You may also want to take the opportunity to welcome the joining together of your family and the groom's.

The father of the bride's speech

Your speech will be made on behalf of both yourself and your partner, as a couple (unless, of course, your partner is giving a speech, too). If your partner has died, this may be the moment to say a few words in her memory and to express your approval of the groom on her behalf, too.

The speech checklist

- In your opening remarks, you can talk about the success of the wedding so far and any amusing incidents.
- Thank everyone for attending, perhaps making a special mention of those people who have travelled long distances.

The speech checklist

• Include stories and remarks about your daughter – how you've watched her grow up and change, your hopes for her and the ways in which she has foiled or surpassed your expectations.

• Follow on with stories and remarks about her and the groom – how he was first introduced to you and your partner, what you thought of him, how your relationship has developed and how you feel he complements your daughter.

THE FATHER OF THE BRIDE

The speech checklist

- Say something about the groom that has surprised you or something that you've learned from him.
- Make sure your comments include your own partner, too — especially if she's not making a speech herself.
- Finish with a toast to the health and happiness of the bride and groom.

Standing in for the father of the bride

Not every bride is able to have her father 'give her away' at the wedding ceremony or make the traditional speech at the reception. The father of the bride may be dead or he may be estranged from his daughter's family. Very often, a close family friend or relative will be asked to stand in for the father of the bride.

Honouring a deceased father

If you're asked to stand in for the bride's
father because he has died, don't be afraid
to mention him in your speech. You'll find
that many people will be missing him and
will expect you to refer to him. It's quite
appropriate for you to say a few words
about the kind of man he was and how he
would feel about the wedding if he were
still alive. In fact, it would probably be
inappropriate if you didn't mention him.

Standing in for an absent father

If you are standing in for the father of the bride because he is absent as a result of divorce or estrangement, it is not always appropriate to mention him in your speech. It may be prudent to pass over the subject, but be sure to check with the wedding party before you write your speech.

Stand-in preparation

If you've been asked to give a speech in good time before the wedding, use the weeks before the big day to get to know the bridal couple a little better. This personal contact will be a great help when you come to actually write and give your speech.

Stand-in speech

The key to a good wedding speech is sincerity. If you're not all that close to the bridal couple, you'll need to start gathering some information. Call any family members and friends who know the couple well and ask them to provide you with information and pictures documenting artistic talent, teenage crushes, academic and professional achievements, and so on, as well as any harmless gossip – anything that will help you personalize your words.

A few short words

If you've been asked to stand in at short notice, no one will blame you for choosing to keep your speech short and simple. As long as you congratulate the newlyweds and wish them well in the future, compliment the bride on her appearance and say all the expected 'thank-yous', you can't go far wrong. In such cases, it can be helpful to remember that a wedding speech is really no more than an extended toast.

The ushers

If you'd been dreading landing the best man's job, then breathe a sigh of relief – your tasks as an usher are not nearly so onerous. Still, it's nice to be asked to be one, and it is more than a token gesture. As a rule of thumb, there is usually a minimum of one usher per 50 guests.

What does an usher do?

As well as making sure you are available for any fittings for your suit (if necessary) and for the stag night, you may be required to attend the wedding rehearsal. This is an excellent opportunity not only to meet the important members of the wedding party, but also to get an understanding of what's going to be happening at the actual ceremony, which is when you perform your most important duties.

What does an usher do?

The ushers answer directly to the best man. Your duties on the day will be relatively light, but you should be available to help out when and where you can. This could mean assisting a wheelchair-bound guest to their place at the venue, slipping away in advance to light the lanterns for a winter wedding procession or even helping to hand round food or drinks.

THE USHERS

What does an usher do?

As an usher, you are a Jeeves-like presence at the wedding, calmly and politely ironing out any last-minute creases and adding greatly to the smooth running of the day. Best of all, you get to escort the bridesmaids during the course of the day!

What to wear

As befits your 'staff status', you and your fellow ushers will want to dress in the style of the groom and best man. So, if the groom is in morning dress, you'll be, too, although perhaps you'll have a flower buttonhole of a different colour from the groom and best man.

The wedding morning

It's a good idea for you and your colleagues to meet at the wedding venue some time before the ceremony and well before the arrival of any early guests. Here, you can collect buttonholes and the service sheets, synchronize watches and discuss any other relevant issues. Bring an umbrella, too, just in case you need to escort guests to and from their transport in the rain.

During the ceremony

Make sure you recognize the 'key players' at the wedding, especially the parents. Having ushers from the bride's side and also from the groom's will greatly help here, as well as contributing in a practical way to the symbolic union of two families, which a wedding represents.

Seating the guests

Ideally, you'll have a seating plan for the front rows (from the best man) and be briefed about any family friction that may need to be negotiated. If there's a chief usher, he will delegate the other tasks, such as giving out the service sheets.

Seating the guests

Be aware of any elderly or disabled guests who could use some help. At least one usher should stand at the back during the service, to welcome latecomers and discreetly guide them to a spare seat. You may also want to make sure parents with small babies are seated near doors, so they can make a quick exit if they need to!

Bride's to the left...

At least one of the ushers will stand at the foot of the aisle to ask guests on which side they are to sit. Don't forget: groom's friends and family on the right, bride's on the left.

Mid-field usher

Another usher will position himself halfway
down the aisle to guide people to their
seats. This is easier said than done, however,
since you'll be trying to get guests with
babies into the aisle seats and directing tall
people to places where they won't be
obscuring other people's views!

Escorting the bride's mother

The chief usher will be posted at the church door to escort the bride's mother to her seat on arrival at the church. She should be the last to take her seat before the entrance of the bridal party.

After the ceremony

Outside the wedding venue, you may be asked to find specific guests for the photographer's pictures, or – more likely – to help organize transport for the guests from the wedding venue to the reception.

At the reception

Once you get to the reception venue, you can start to relax a little and enjoy the party, although if jobs need doing, be ready to lend a hand – perhaps to help with the efficient flow of food and drink. When the guests arrive at the reception, direct them to the room where the bride and groom would like them to assemble. If traditional dancing takes place, you may be required to dance with the bridesmaids for the second dance.

Top tips

What would be the advice of other grooms, fathers of the bride, best men and ushers who have already performed their wedding roles?

Pre-wedding organization
The groom

- Make sure you know how your outfit works – your bride won't be around to tie your cravat for you!
- Spend some quality time with your bride doing something – anything – that's not to do with planning your wedding.
- Do a practice run from wherever you are spending the night before the wedding to the ceremony venue, so you can gauge what the traffic will be like on the day.

MEN AT WEDDINGS

Pre-wedding organization
The father of the bride

- Make sure you know what you'll be paying for – you don't want any surprise bills!
- You and, if applicable, the mother of the bride will be going to the ceremony in bridal cars – make sure you have made plans for getting home from the reception.
- No matter how neurotic you think your daughter is about this wedding, be there to lend her a hand, an ear and a shoulder to cry on!

Pre-wedding organization
The best man

- Don't let the stag night plans come as a complete surprise to the groom. He might have promised the bride he wouldn't go to Blackpool, so don't make him break that promise.

- Practise your speech in front of your mother or aunt. If you can't say it in front of them, it's probably not appropriate.

- Try to meet up with the bride beforehand to check with her what she expects of you.

Pre-wedding organization
The ushers

- Ensure you are available for suit fittings, the stag night, the rehearsal and the wedding day!

- If possible, introduce yourself to the parents of the bride and groom in advance so you all know who you are!

- Don't get too carried away the night before. It's a long day and you won't enjoy it with a hangover.

The ceremony

Essential thoughts for the father of the bride
Travelling to the church with your daughter
is the only time you'll have alone together
during the day. Think about what you want
to say to her during this time.

Essential thoughts for the groom
Relax during the ceremony. This is about
your marriage, not whether Auntie Mabel
can hear you from the back.

The ceremony

Dos and don'ts for the best man

- Do remember the rings, whatever you do. This can't be underlined enough.
- Don't forget the rings. It won't be as funny as it was in *Four Weddings and a Funeral*.

The ceremony
Tips for the ushers

- Keep tissues and a local taxi firm number handy for emergencies.
- Make sure everyone has switched off their mobile phones, pagers and bleepers.
- Leave the ceremony last, in order to ensure everyone has transport to the reception venue.

At the reception
The groom

- Take your cue for the events of the day from the bride.
- The day will fly by quickly, so take the time to step back and let it all sink in on a few occasions.
- You may want to have an extra shirt to hand, just in case you spill wine or drop wedding cake down your front!

At the reception
The father of the bride

- If you're going to tell childhood anecdotes in your speech, run them past the bride's mother or best friend, to check you aren't going to embarrass your daughter!
- Make sure you're available for photographs when needed.
- If you're paying for the reception, make sure you know whether you're expected to settle the bill at the end of the evening.

At the reception
The best man

• Your speech comes last, but make sure you've had only the one drink for Dutch courage before it's your turn to give it. Ten drinks do not make you ten times funnier.

• If you are seriously nervous about speaking, read out the telegrams first, so that you get used to speaking aloud.

• Don't forget to compliment the bride in your speech!

At the reception
The usher

- Keep an eye out for anyone who looks like they might get a little tipsy and cause a problem. A quiet word in their ear or the ear of a companion, reminding them where they are, should do the trick.

- If the dancing is slow to get going, ask some of the bridesmaids to dance.

- If you decorate the couple's room or car, make sure that it won't upset them or be considered criminal damage!

ABOUT CONFETTI.CO.UK

Confetti.co.uk is the UK's leading wedding and special occasion website, helping more than 100,000 brides, grooms and guests every month.

To find out more or to order your confetti.co.uk gift book or party brochure, visit www.confetti.co.uk, call 0870 840 6060, or e-mail us at info@confetti.co.uk

Other books in this series include *Wedding Readings*; *The Wedding Book of Calm*; *Compatibility*; *Confettiquette*; *Speeches* and the comprehensive *Wedding Planner*.